ALL YOU WANTED

Hypr

SUMEET SHARMA

New Dawn

NEW DAWN
a division of Sterling Publishers (P) Ltd.
A-59, Okhla Industrial Area, Phase-II, New Delhi-110020
Tel : 6313023, 6320118, 6916209, 6916165
E-mail : ghai@nde.vsnl.net.in
www.sterlingpublishers.com

All You Wanted to Know About - Hypnosis
© 1999, Sterling Publishers Private Limited
ISBN 81 207 2271 x
Reprint 2001

Published by Sterling Publishers Pvt. Ltd., New Delhi-110020.
Lasertypeset by Vikas Compographics, New Delhi-110020.
Printed at Sai Printers, New Delhi.

Contents

4

Preface

A lot of water has flown under the bridge since my first book "Reiki and Hypnosis for success and self-realisation". My special gratitude goes to M/s. **Sterling Publishers Pvt. Ltd., New Delhi** for publishing this book.

Under the stewardship of my Reiki Master, Dipti Gandhi we opened the **Holistic Healing Centre.** The Centre offers healing services using most of the Spiritual Healing therapies such as Reiki, Pranic,

Magnified, Aroma therapy, Acupressure, Crystals, Pyramids, Music therapy and Hypnosis too. Already over 400 patients have been given various combination treatment. The success rate has been close to cent per cent especially in the case of chronic and psychosomatic disorders like diabetes, backaches, eczema, migraines, allergic asthma, cancer, etc, to name a few.

A special thanks to my Reiki Master, Dipti Gandhi and Swami Sukhabodhananda who have played a vital role in changing my entire perception of life.

Life has become very hectic, attending to one's work in office and looking after the Centre in the evenings and holding workshops every weekend. But we have taken a positive attitude that we will serve the society by helping people to "HEAL THEMSELVES BY SHOWING THEM THE RIGHT PATH".

Topography of the Human Brain

"There is nothing great about earth except man, there is nothing great about man except his mind."

Sir William Hamilton

The above statement can be further expanded to say that it is the human mind alone, which can fantasise and conjure up castles in the air. New scanners have made it possible to explore the living brain. As one prods deeper into its intricacy, it appears more marvellous .

Figure 1: Parts of the Human Brain

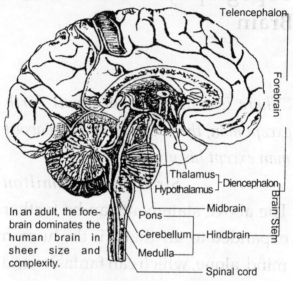

In an adult, the forebrain dominates the human brain in sheer size and complexity.

Human brain is divided into 3 parts as per neuro scientist. Paul Macleen, who compared human brain to that of animals. Some animals like cats and dogs have keen sense of smell and hearing which cannot be duplicated by humans.

The first part of the brain is a structure at the top of the spinal cord, including portions of the brain's stem. This resembles the brain of reptiles called *Reptilian*. This regulates breathing, heartbeat, muscle movements and other basic instincts.

The second part is the limbic system which is well developed in all mammals but not in reptiles and contributes to the additional qualities like snarling, purring, growling, showing affection and guilt hence this section is called the *Mammalian Brain*.

The third part is the outer bulges of the cerebrum and the overlying cerebral cortex which is the *Reasoning Brain*.

The human cerebral cortex is further distinguished by its folds, valleys and ridges which increases the surface area of the cortex and allows maximum area of grey matter to be packed within the confines of the skull. The power of speech, observation, analysis etc. makes humans different from the other living things.

The cerebral cortex is covered by grey tissue containing billions of neurons which is called **"grey**

matter". We often term intelligent people as having more grey Botanically this is not true because a person with more grey matter need not necessarily be more intelligent.

Messages from the brain are sent, received and stored by a wonderful network of nervous or nerve cells that employ a unique blend of chemistry and electricity yet to be duplicated by man. Brain is divided into four lobes by phrenologists, and each lobe has a specific function. One lobe can take over the function of another, if it is damaged.

Figure 2: Lobes of the Human Brain.

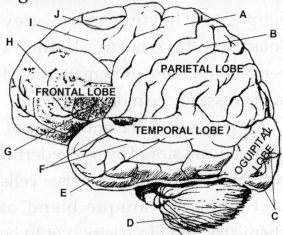

A - Motor Cortex: at the back of the frontal lobe, controlling voluntary muscles.

B - Somatosensory Cortex a: the front of the parietal lobe, receiving and interpreting signals from all senses.

C - Vision Centers: receiving and interpreting visual signals.

D - Cerebellum

E - Wernicke's Area: understanding speech and other sensory information

F - Hearing Centers

G - Broca's Area: (usually in left hemisphere) controls muscles that produce speech.

H - Prefrontal Cortex: reasoning, planning, emotions

I - Premotor Cortex: skilled coordination involving many muscles

J - Supplementary Motor Area

Hypothalamus is the **Brain of the Brain** and surprisingly this is no bigger than the tip of your thumb yet it rules the entire endocrine system. The endrocrine system is a collection of ductless gland throughout the body that secrete hormones directly into the blood stream. These glands include the pituitary, thyroid, thymus, adrenals, pancreas, ovaries and testes. Their job is to control the internal environment of each organ and cell of the body.

A meager task of lifting the hand involves millions of messages sent via billions of nerve cells to and from your brain. The thinking part of the brain decides to lift the hand, messages go out to the motor nerves that serve your hand, these are aided through information by way of optic nerve. Life without autonomic nervous system would be a total chaos.

Some yoga practitioners can, however, override the autonomic system to lower their heartbeat, body temperature, metabolism to almost stop during meditation which can last for days or months.

The idea is to give readers an insight into the phenomenal responsibilities and functions the brain.

Some scientists have separated brain by terming it as physical entity and mind as the soul.

Albert Einstein said, "The most beautiful experience we can have is of the mysterious. It is the fundamental emotion which stands at the cradle of true art and true science. Whoever does not know it and can no longer wonder is as good as dead. A knowledge of the existence of something we cannot penetrate, our perceptions of the profoundest reason and in the most primitive form are accessible to our minds. It is this knowledge and the emotion that constitute true religiosity."

Life and its Effect on Human Psychology

"Man is an animal that makes bargains, no other animal does this, one dog does not change its bone with another."

Adam Smith

Right from the time we are born we need security and warmth which is given by our mothers. As the child grows, it starts taking note of things and people around it and instinctively starts imitating them and harbours the same good or bad habits of his parents or guardians.

The famous psychologist, Sigmund Freud, placed most of the responsibilities for emotional problems on childhood experience.

During the formative years of the child between 12 and 18 years, parents and others have to be very careful how they talk and behave in the presence of the children as during this period anything negative gets absorbed quickly by them. Since their mind can be easily moulded into whatever shape desired.

We see all kinds of people around us with good and bad behaviour. Anger, lust, jealousy, envy, hatred and ego are bad emotions but these are only the effect. All of us have read Newton's third law of motion, "Every action has an equal and opposite reaction". This applies to human nature as every action has a cause behind it.

Other character disorders are phobias, obsessions, compulsive behaviour, hysteria, excessive alcoholism, sexual desires, drug addiction, anxiety, fatigue, inferiority complex, immature behaviour and other psychosomatic disorders.

Psychosomatic disease seem to stem from subconscious problems situation and words rather than actual infections or injuries. Some of the examples of these illness are as follows:

• Allergies and sinus, eczema and hives, obesity and constipation, lack of appetite, haemorrhoids, peptic ulcer, asthma, blood pressure, bed wetting, migraine, alcoholism, hiccups, drug addiction, impotence, premature ejaculation, retarded ejaculation, vaginitis, infertility, frigidity and menstrual cramps.

Stress and tension serve to lower bodily resistance so we become more susceptible to infections and disease. So it is said that all illnesses have an emotional background.

Why do we fall ill?

- Unresolved guilt, grief or anger following a tragedy can give rise to illness viz. self punishment.

- Stress and bitterness due to caring for a now deceased loved one can cause illness that is an escape from despair.

- Illness can provide an escape from unhappiness specially if one is not happy at home or place of work.

- A disregarded plea for help or a divorce may lead to illness in the heart-broken partner.

- Families may unknowingly want member to be ill because by doing so there is balance and happiness amongst members of the family.

- Illness can be means of manipulating loved ones even by allowing the ill person to be dependent and cared for and thus keeping a family member from leaving the home front.

- Illness can also be a source of punishment to those with whom we are angry including ourselves.

- Illness can help one to escape from boredom, loss of meaning and self-worth. The examples of such illness would be the abandoning of home by children, retirement, living in poverty and unemployment.

23

- A destroyed or faulty picture embedded in one's mind can lead to the belief that illness and death would visit one at a particular age as similar thing has happened to another family member.

When one can recognise oneself in these situations one can surely escape illness and death as well by choosing life. One's present is often due to one's choice and one is fully responsible for one's own health and life. Therefore, one should believe in one's ability to influence the circumstances one finds in life.

The Sub conscious Mind — the treasure within you

"The mind is its own place and in itself can make a heaven of hell and hell of heaven."

John Milton (Paradise Lost).

Let us try and understand the functioning of the left and right side of the brain.

Left side	**Right side**
Conditioned	*The Subconscious linked to Super-conscious*
• Active	* Imaginative

- Assertive
- Logical
- Deducive
- Rational
- Male aspects of character

* Intuitive
* Receptive
* Clairvoyant
* Sadness
* Female aspects of character

We are all aware that we have an inner mind which is called 'subliminal', 'subjective', 'id' or the subconscious mind. Freud was one of the first who gave an insight into the functioning of the subconscious mind linking it with the causes of various diseases. Dr Carl Jung, the Swiss psychiatrist, termed the spiritual part of the mind as superconscious which was directly connected to God.

The subconscious mind works like a computer. The subconscious mind inspires, guides and is a permanent store house of memory. Our mind remembers everything we see, feel and experience but to recall is difficult. It is said that the subconscious mind has a memory capacity of 70-100 trillion images because all our feelings, emotions and experiences are stored within us as an image or sound. Just as a computer digitises everything, our brain too does the same.

Subconscious mind never sleeps, never rests and is always on duty because it controls our heartbeat, circulation of blood, regulates digestion, assimilates, harmonises and eliminates. It controls all the vital processes and functions of our body and knows the answers to all our problems.

The objective mind learns from observation, experience, education and its great function is reasoning, whereas the subjective mind performs its highest function when our objective senses are in abeyance.

Thoughts are conveyed via the conscious mind to the subconscious by impression made in the brain cells like an image or a movie. It uses every bit of information gathered in our life time and draws all the energy and wisdom within us to bring solutions to our problems.

Suppose one had been bitten by a dog at the age of 10, one will continue to be scared of dogs for the rest of his/her life viewing it from the childhood experience. This is because our subconscious mind remembers the incident. The conscious mind may forget but the subconscious mind remembers in greatest detail unless the event is cancelled from the memory.

Subconscious mind is always awake whether one is asleep,

unconscious, under drug or alcohol effect or under coma. One of its functions is to guard us from harm and danger, yet ironically it also causes illness and even self destruction.

Subconscious mind is infinite intelligence possessed by man beyond time and space, and it helps us to receive new thoughts, ideas, business plans, discoveries, inventions, and knowledge of nature.

Subconscious mind has the habit of taking everything literally. If we keep on thinking that we will never succeed in a particular venture, it is most likely that we will not because we are blocking all positive energy flow into the subconscious. This results only in negative energy getting attracted. Therefore, it is we who are responsible for our successes and failures in life.

If we have conveyed an erroneous concept to our subconscious mind the method of overcoming it is by repetition of constructive and harmonious thoughts, positive attitude and visualising a happy ending rather than negative thoughts and suggestions.

Doctors have recognised this fact about the mind hence, however complex the operation maybe, they keep on encouraging the patients just before an operation.

During the post operative period visitors are not allowed near the patient because any negative suggestion given will go deep into the patient's subconscious mind thereby damaging whatever had been done to rectify the patient's state of health through the operation.

It is very important that we do not use negative suggestions with growing children as it gets rooted in their subconscious mind and reflects later in his/her behaviour. This effect can be seen in their behaviour, hostility, anxiety, lack of confidence, etc. Whatever one believes in one's mind is what we experience physically in the outside world. We have two sides of life objective-subjective, visible-invisible, thought-manifestation.

Even prayers and beliefs are positive signals which we give to our subconscious mind as something acceptable and true. The thought which is acceptable as true will automatically execute itself. When we believe we are healthy we will remain healthy as our subconscious mind keeps our immune system in perfect condition.

Bhagwan Sathya Sai Baba says "Faith is the root of tree of mankind on which it survives".

Faith is the starting point of our spiritual and mental progress. In India we can find umpteen examples of faith, belief and superstitions. These can be explained scientifically whereas many are blindly followed. Faith and belief which are for our own and universal good are acceptable. However, faith which brings injury to others, either mental or physical is not acceptable.

Baba said we should develop a sense of *Viveka* (discrimination) which will help us to demarcate good and bad things. This demarcation comes from *Jnana* (knowledge). A child who utters bad words may not know the meaning of it hence one should explain the meaning of the word to him so that he does not repeat it.

While praying we do not give any thoughts to negative conditions. This attitude of mind brings a harmonious union of conscious and subconscious mind which releases the healing power.

In India, we frequently visit temples and shrines and pray. Temples and holy places have positive energies due to the repetition of God's name, songs, mantras, etc, which soothe our mind. We feel calm and respond in these places with openness. Our subconscious mind unfolds the knot of our problems and gives us the solutions.

During every moment of our life we harbour more negative energies than positive one. Whatever we see around us makes an impact on the subconscious mind and remains deep rooted till reprogramming is done.

Dr. Bruce Goldberg in his book has proved that subconscious mind does not only have memory a of our present life but also of the past lives. The subconscious mind may not want us to know anything of the past as per the wisdom it possesses and may decide not to give us any information at all of the past lives that may affect our present life.

However, by scientific hypnosis and past life regression, anyone can go back and witness their life as it was.

Some people having peculiar behavioural problems, have been regressed to their past lives to find the cause of the problem in their present life. When the cause is healed the problem disappears instantly.

Subconscious mind never grows old. It is ageless, timeless and endless. Hence it is very important to develop patience, kindness, humility, will power, responsibility for oneself, peace, harmony, hope and brotherly love towards every creation of GOD.

The subconscious mind can be dealt with creative visualisation, positive affirmations and self-hypnosis to bring harmony and balance in all aspects of your life.

How negative attitudes affect a person

- One parent used to tell his child almost everyday, "You will become a useless person and never become something in life." When the child became an adult, he was a failure in all aspects of life. Finally, he became a priest and found solace. Parents should be cautious and not use any negative words or commands while dealing with their children.

- A teacher used to motivate his pupils by saying, "Try and try again, you will succeed. Work hard and pray to God for success."

Thus his student turned out to be toppers in academics and brought many laurels to the school. The encouraging words of the teacher worked like magic. (It is better to keep on encouraging, rewarding and praising the children for slightest good done by them. After all there is a deep desire within all of us to be appreciated.

- A widow used to tell her daughter after puberty to be careful of men as they were cheats, opportunists and sex maniacs. This influenced her and she hated men till her late thirties until she met a loving and caring man. She let go of her mother's influence. (The mother had spoilt an innocent child's attitude towards men just because she herself was a victim of terrible experiences).

- A young boy when caught masturbating by his father was told that he would become insane. That boy became impotent. Later his problem vanished after scientific counselling and reassurance. (Often impotence is not an organic defect but arises due to deep emotional guilt which can be easily cured by reprogramming the subconscious mind through positive affirmations.)

- A man met with an accident and fractured his leg. He happened to overhear his doctor saying that he would never be normal again and that he would always limp. This man although clinically certified to be fit, walked with a limp until he met a mind trainer who succeeded in cancelling the negative thought from his mind.

There are innumerable examples to prove beyond doubt that subconscious mind remembers the past life as well as present. There is chance that our conscious mind may sometimes forget certain incidences but our subconscious mind remembers everything. It also causes all the emotional and physical disorders arising due to these deep rooted memories.

Any passing comments or trivial statements can have a devastating effect on our subconscious mind because it is not argumentative or analytical. It accepts all the statements directly on the face value.

It is very imperative that we do not become sad and depressed as negative thoughts crowd the subconscious mind which could react immediately or maybe after several years. It is the responsibility of elders and parents to be very careful in using words when they are amidst children in the formative years as during this time the mind takes concrete shape for many years to come.

Some positive tips for perennial happiness:

- If someone has hurt you physically or verbally, forgive him or her.
- If someone tries to belittle you ignore them.

- If someone you advise does not wish to listen to you, leave that person to face his own fate.
- If you help someone, do not expect anything in return. Conflicts between spouses or parent-children arises due to very high expectations.
- If you have a special talent or God gift do not become egoistic and haughty about it or consider yourself superior to others.
- If someone is jealous of you and your achievements, sympathise with them.
- Learn to channelise your desire into higher creativity and

consciousness by adopting meditation.

- Keep away from malice as they will not give you perpetual happiness.
- Learn to set new goals in life as this will keep your life interesting and full of zeal and zest.

Baba says, "Life is a challenge, face it. Life is love, enjoy it. Life is a song, sing it". Love is the common denominator for all maladies in life. So we need to develop unconditional love for everything — our work, profession, family, neighbours, GOD, and people we meet socially.

Technique of self-hypnosis

The word "hypnos" means sleep in Greek. The first student of modern hypnotism was Dr. James Braid (1795-1880), a Scottish surgeon. He used the techniques of mesmerism in a scientific way and coined the word "Hypnosis". He developed a technique of suggestions given to the patients and cured them. However, his method was misused by police officials.

In early 1800, James Esdaile, performed painless operations

without the use of any anaesthesia during his practice in Calcutta, India. Later John Elliotson, Jean Martin Charcot, Sigmund Freud added further dimensions to the use of hypnosis in medicine, neurology and psychoan-alysis.

It was Freud who first recognised that our nervous habits or neurosis is due to the subconscious mind. The popularity of hypnosis grew many folds in the UK and the USA, mainly in the field of painless dentistry and childbirth.

What is Hypnosis?

Hypnosis is a state of mind where our conscious mind goes into a trance and suggestions are given to the subconscious mind directly which does not argue but accepts the suggestion at its face value.

We are neither asleep nor awake nor unconscious, in fact our mind is more alert and completely aware of our surroundings. Our body is completely relaxed. We hypnotise ourselves unknowingly several times in a day while doing day to day activities. This is how our body learns to relax otherwise we would die of stress at a very early age.

Myths about Hypnotism

Most people think that under the hypnotic state one would reveal all the secrets and the hypnotist would take advantage of it later. This is not true because in the hypnotic state our mind is more alert and will not reveal any information which we do not wish to reveal.

A myth, especially amongst the ladies is that hypnotist may molest them under hypnotic spell. Again this is not true because one is in complete control of oneself and can come out of the spell any time if one does not like the suggestions given by the hypnotist.

Some people believe that one becomes unconscious and may not come out of hypnosis. This is a myth and no one under hypnosis has ever lost consciousness. Some people take a longer time to come out of the spell due to the fact that they enjoy the state of relaxation. They come out on their free will when they really feel so.

Positive use of Hypnotism

The subconscious mind takes things as it is and hypnotism is one tool we can use to directly communicate with our subconscious mind and use it for the good of ourselves and others.

Hypnotism and auto suggestion can be used to:

- remove fears and phobias
- give up bad habits and addictions
- increase stamina and vitality
- eliminate emotional problems and depressions
- cure psychosomatic illness
- overcome inferiority complex and other behavioural problems
- conquer pain
- lose weight and stay trim
- improve marital and sex life

- overcome allergies and other common ailments
- develop positive attitude in life
- manifest goals in our life
- creation of wealth and property
- to improve self confidence
- overcome stress
- cure stammering and stuttering
- for entertainment purpose
- to regress people's age and past life

Hypnotism has more positive application than negative ones.

Levels of Hypnosis

There are 3 main stages in hypnosis:

- **Lethargic or light hypnotic sleep.**

Here one experiences light slumber and dullness and one feels very relaxed and comfortable. One is told to visualise events; past events can be recalled and suggestions given.

- **Hallucinatory or medium state.** When relaxation experienced under lethargic state continues, the hypnotist gives further suggestions to take the person to this state where visualisation is more accurate and one can be asked to forget the past trauma or give up addictions or to cancel trauma and addiction from the memory.

- **Somnambulistic or deep state.**
  It is a similar state to sleep walking. Although this state is not required for treatment it is often used in stage hypnosis for entertainment purpose.

  If suggestions like "you cannot move your hand and your body is stiff now" is given during hypnotism then the effect is really felt till the hypnotist removes the command. Past life regressions can also be done in this sate.

  Complete anesthesia amnesia, control of body function, positive and negative hallucination of the five senses, time distortion and ability to open ones eyes without being awake is possible in this state.

There is still a deeper state called plenary trance but it takes several hours and is impossible to reach by self hypnosis.

How to do self-hypnosis?

- Select a quiet place and ensure that no one disturbs you.
- Keep an object at your eye level and continuously stare at it. You can also use a candle to start with.
- Take three deep breaths and suggest to yourself, mentally, "as I stare at this object, my eyes will become heavier and heavier and I will not be able to keep them open. I am going into self hypnosis for 10 minutes." The time can vary depending on you.

- Your eyes will automatically close then say mentally," I am totally relaxed now." Gradually relax all the parts of the body.
  Then say "All my muscles in the body are totally relaxed and I cannot move them even if I want to." At this stage you are in the lethargic state.
- Imagine yourself standing on the top of staircase and as you climb down the staircase count backwards and you will go deeper and deeper into a trance.
- Now if you have done the above exercise correctly you are in state

59

II and you can visualise yourself at a place where you get maximum peace of mind. This could be your most favourite place perhaps your own room, temple, an imaginary hill, lake or a scenic spot.

• There is no harm in staying in this state for long. Link this spot with a trigger word like. 'utopia,' 'secret,' 'spot', 'place,' 'tranquility' anything you like.

Whenever you are self-hypnotised, repeating any of the above words will immediately take you to the same spot painted by your mind and permanently accepted by your subconscious mind.

When you want to come out of hypnosis tell yourself "As I count 3 to 1, I will come out of self-hypnosis feeling fresh, revitalised and full of energy."

This is very important because if you suddenly open your eyes you may feel dazed or have a slight headache.

- Count to yourself
  Count 1 "slowly coming out"
  Count 2 "coming out"
  Count 3 "wide and awake"

You will notice that you will feel rejuvenated. Light music in the background helps you to relax better. It is not necessary to go to level 3 during self hypnosis as affirmations given at stage 2 itself go very deep into the subconscious mind.

How to hypnotise others

The person you are trying to hypnotise should have full faith in you. He must be willing to surrender as all hypnosis is self hypnosis. If the person is not cooperative his conscious mind would interfere and cause impediments in relaxation due to which hypnosis will not take place at all. A lot of faith building exercise has to be done by the hypnotist including the prior consent of the subject in order to succeed.

Another caution for male hypnotist hypnotising a female

subject is that he should keep another lady in the room during the hypnosis sessions.

It is better to remove any doubts or fears with respect to hypnotism prior to taking the subject into trance, this will help them relax better.

- Select a quiet place and ensure that no one disturbs.
- Instruct the subject to take deep breaths and say "as you take 3 deep breaths you will feel very calm and relaxed".
- The tone of the hypnotist should be soothing and firm and not commanding as it will not help the subject to relax.

"Now your legs and toes are relaxed."

"Now your chin is relaxed."

"Now your thighs are relaxed."

"Now your abdomen is relaxed."

"Now your chest is relaxed."

"Now your neck muscles are relaxed."

"Now your chin and jaws are relaxed."

- "Imagine yourself standing on the top of a staircase and as you go down from the top step you are getting more and more relaxed."

- Count backwards from 10 slowly "As you reach step 1 you will be deeply relaxed, so relaxed that you cannot move the muscles of your body even if you want to." By this time your subject will be in stage 1.

- "Now I am taking you to your favourite place where you will find mental peace and tranquillity." Slowly describe the place and keep your voice soothing. "Imagine you are in the place where there are hills around you, birds are chirping and lot of greenery around you. Now smell the flowers and the fresh earthy smell. You are enjoying this scenery painted by your mind."

- Attach a trigger word to this imagined spot by saying "I am giving you a trigger word Utopia, secret spot, mental place. Select any word "Whenever you want to relax in future, just close your eyes, take 3 deep breaths. Relax and repeat the trigger word."

This will go deep into the subject's subconscious mind and remain there throughout his life. It is imperative that you repeat the word at least 3-5 times to ensure that the subconscious mind gets the message.

- Then say, "I leave you to enjoy this scenery as long as you want and I shall keep quiet for 5 min." The subject under trance looses track of time. So after the given time you can bring the subject back.
- You can take the subject deeper into the trance by saying, "Now with every breath you breathe you are going deeper and deeper into a trance."

By this you can take them to stage II and even III of hypnosis and give suggestions which will be useful to them and will go directly in to their subconscious mind.

- You can test the level of hypnotic stage by telling the subject, "Now I will instruct you to lift your hand up but it is so heavy that you cannot lift it, the more you try the harder it will become."

If the subject is in a deep trance he or she will not be able to move. Otherwise those who are not can easily lift their hands. It is not always possible to hypnotise everyone as it all depends on how good the subjects are at relaxing themselves. Self confidence and experience of hypnotist to handle difficult people is important and variations depend on the person.

All positive suggestions can be given at this stage.

- To bring the subject out of hypnosis say,

"As I count to 3 you will come out feeling fresh, revitalised, full of energy and feeling better than before."

"Count 1- slowly coming out."

"Count 2 -coming out."

"Count 3 -wide awake now."

- Some subject may take longer to come out of trance after repeating the above words. There is no cause for panic. Some hypnotists leave them to come out on their own.

In very rare cases, they may not come out, then you should say, "I know you are enjoying this state of relaxation. If I want you will never be able to experience this state of relaxation in the future, I have the power and you know I can do it." Say it firmly.

As explained before subjects under hypnosis will never do anything against their wishes or what they dislike so giving this command will bring them out instantly.

It is helpful to use music as it helps the subject to relax better.

Creative Visualisation

Human mind runs in many directions at the same time and cannot be still for a second. Only when the mind is made to focus on one thing can eternal peace be obtained and anything be achieved by us.

Visualisation is nothing but pictures in our mind to train the mind and manifest any kind of goals. Creative visualisation involves 3 steps.

• Setting a goal

- Learning to relax
- Visualising a successful outcome

Why visualisation works

Visualising specific moments, images, pictures, performance and techniques endeavour to create patterns in our brain. The more we visualise the more ingrained these neutral pattern becomes.

Since it is the brain which tells the muscles what to do, when and how to move the patterns the more perfect the movement become.

When we use affirmation along with visualisation the message

73

directly goes to the subconscious mind which in turn conveys it to the superconscious and man can reach any heights if this technique is done correctly.

Many sportsman all over the world have used this technique to excel themselves in their own field. One of the example is *Jim Thorpe*, who was born on May 28, 1888 and was one of the greatest all round athlete known to mankind till date. He was a member of the USA Olympic team in 1912. He won 10 gold medals in various sports. The special gift he possessed was his keen concentration and ability to visualise all games and competition well in advance.

The famous golfer, *Jack Nicklous*, ranked as the best golfer for over two decades used to imagine the flight of the ball and its trajectory before hitting it.

Olympic gold medalist, swimmer and diver, *Grey Louganis* used visualisation power as part of his preparation for every dive.

As explained before the right hemisphere of our brain is in charge of creativity which organises, finds patterns in events and responds emotionally. Imagination and ideas are fired by the right side of the brain. The right and left brain communicate through corpus callous a thick bundle of nerve fibres in the two halves.

As mentioned above sportsman have used creativity to excel in their area and well-known scientists, inventors and discoverers have reconfirmed their success rate due to their power of visualisation. It is their power of creativity due to which we are enjoying the luxury of air planes, rockets, vacuum cleaners, washing machines and cellular phones.

Some positive affirmations which work

"*Whenever mind wanders, restless and diffuse in its search for satisfaction without, lead it within, train it to rest in the self. Abiding joy comes to those who still the mind. Freeing themselves from the taint of self-will, with their consciousness, they become one with God.*"

Bhagvat Gita
6.18-27

Subconscious mind reaps things in practical life as per the thoughts you sow. Every thought is a cause and every condition is an effect. If one has to be happy one should cease believing in false beliefs, opinions, superstitions and fears and have a strong belief in the strength of his own mind which will bring forth results. Your subconscious mind takes the orders you give it based on what your conscious mind believes and accepts as true.

Subconscious mind works by thought patterns given by the conscious mind and uses every bit of knowledge that you have gathered in your life time to bring about its purpose. It draws on the infinite power and wisdom within you sometimes it brings about immediate solutions and at other times it may take days, weeks or even longer. No one has still fully understood its way of working.

As mentioned earlier subconscious mind does not argue and accepts suggestions as it is. It can be destructive too resulting in misery, failure, suffering, sickness and disaster.

It is very important to develop good constructive thoughts by being spiritual and having strong faith in God and repeated positive affirmations.

Prayer is the starting point of stilling the mind on a single thought and our repeated prayers are nothing but positive affirmations to our subconscious mind because when we visit the temple or church or any place of worship, we rarely have negative thoughts due to the feeling of strong faith and trust. Hence all problems and solutions are within us.

Bhagwan Sri Satya Sai Baba has repeatedly said that "God is not in any temple or church but within us, he dwells in our hearts and minds, only you should discover *Him* by discipline and meditation."

Listed below are some positive affirmations one can give to oneself after going into self-hypnosis. The procedure for self-hypnosis is described and these affirmations will be more effective if done separately every time. Hence one should go into hypnosis, relax and give auto suggestions for at least five times and come out then go in again for second affirmation.

A wise thing would be to list out all your problems, desires and objects of fantasy, and put them in order of priority before proceeding.

- To have *Positive Attitude* : "I am self reliant, self controlled, filled with independence and determination. I have great inner courage and project a positive self image. I am confident, optimistic and enthusiastic and look forward to new challenges and emerge as a winner."

- To *eliminate stress* : "I am at ease. I am at peace with myself, the world and everyone around me. I am physically and emotionally relaxed and in complete balance and harmony. Ultimate relaxation is mine, I am relaxed, I am relaxed." (repeat this five times)

- *Wealth* and *Success* : "I have a desire to be wealthy and become wealthy. My creative thinking opens the door of the monastery of abundance. What I imagine is, what I create. I am persistent, ambitious and determined."

- *Weight Loss* : "I am slim, trim, and lead a healthy lifestyle. I eat only healthy, nutritious food in small portions and stick to my diet. I now weigh so and so kgs and achieved it without any side effects."

- *Health* and *Healing* : "Day by day in every way I am becoming

83

healthier and healthier. My immune system functions at optimum efficiency and keeps me in good health. I choose perfect health and use the unlimited power of my mind to heal myself."

- *Accelerate Learning* : "I have the ability to focus my energy concentration to accelerate healing. I am developing photographic memory and remember what I learn, I remain alert and focused and can instantly compare data."

- *Self-Discipline* : "I have the self-discipline to accomplish personal and professional goals. I direct my time and energy to manifest my desires and increase my self-discipline. I am taking control of my life and am committed to my goals."
- *Self-Esteem* : "I am self-confident. I believe in my abilities and enjoy high self-esteem. My positive self-image generates success and happiness. I am proud of myself and do things that make me proud."
- *Goal Accomplishment* : "I have the power to do more things in

less time. I am increasing my speed and productivity. My time is valuable and I use it efficiently to accomplish my goals fully."

- *Addictions Removal* : "I have the will-power and discipline to do anything I desire. I ignore all cravings and insecurity. I am letting go of the past, freeing myself and enjoy a deep inner peace and love for myself."

- *Brain Power* : "Day by day my mind is becoming agile and alert. My learning abilities and performance is increasing daily. I think more clearly and creatively."

- *Self-Confidence* : "I am reliant, self confident, full of independence and determination. I have great courage and project very positive self-image. Every day I am becoming more self-confident."

- *Psychic Ability* : " Day by day my phychic abilities are opening up. I am able to develop my extra sensory perceptions and sixth sense. I am telepathic and clairvoyant."

- *Enhance Creativity* : "Day by day I am becoming more and more creative. I draw creative inspiration from the universe and release unlimited power of my creative ability and so I am creative."

- *Develop Charisma* : "I project an inner warmth and genuine friendliness. I am self-aroused and independent. I am becoming a charismatic person."
- *Quick Thinking* : "I get what I want with quick thinking. I instantly respond with best answers. I am mentally alert and focused all the times. I think and react quickly to problems. I am releasing the full power of my mind."

- *Powerful Personality* : "Day by day in every way I am becoming more aware of my inner strength. I am able to unleash my potential to direct and lead others. I have the power and ability to attain my goals. I am a powerful negotiator and get what I want. I am forceful and dynamic as required in situations." Use *power* as trigger word.

- *Inner Peace*: "I am at peace with myself and the world and everyone in it. I accept the things I cannot change in life. My mind is like calm water and that's all I need. I now feel peaceful, balanced and harmonious and experience tranquillity, love and joy." Use *peace, balance* and *harmony* as trigger words.

- *Satisfaction* and *Happiness* : "I create my own space for satisfaction and happiness in my life. I accept what I cannot change and change what I can. I have the power and ability to create any reality I desire to live. I am happy and satisfied." Use *believe* and *achieve* as key words.
- *Insomnia* : "I am sleeping peacefully through the night.

Peaceful sleep has become a reality. I fall asleep early and sleep well. I wake up relaxed and refreshed. I can go to sleep at will." *Peaceful sleep* is the trigger word.

- **Remove Pain** : "Day by day and everyday my discomfort is getting less. I am relaxed and feel good. I am mentally healing myself and being healed. With every breath I am healed and the pain is less. I am feeling great" *Relax* and *release* are the trigger words.

You can use specific part like back or headache in your above affirmations if you like for faster results.

- *Forgive* and *Forget* : "I forgive and release my anger and expectations. I allow negativity to flow through me without affecting me. Everyday I find it easier to forgive and release my expectations of others I am liberating myself." *Forgive* and *release* are the trigger words.

- *Creative Visualisation* : "I am visualising what I want. I see it in my mind and set it to manifest. I can visualise my dreams into reality. I hold a clear picture in my mind and combine it with emotional desire."

- *Guilt Release* : "I am peaceful with myself and my past. I have forgiven myself. I learn from the past to create a positive future. Everyday I am at peace with myself. I am feeling better and better all over." Use *peaceful mind* as a trigger word.

- *Worry* and *Fear* : "I am confident and secure. I am calm and optimistic. I feel powerful and in full control of myself. I am peaceful, balanced and harmonious. My mind is calm and thinks positive thoughts. I am in control of my life."

- *Miracle Manifestation* : "This week I will manifest a miracle in my life. I am open to any miracle big or small which will change my life in a positive way. I receive what I desire. I live in abundance."

- *Alcohol addiction* : "I have stopped drinking. I have the inner strength to turn away from alcohol. I have stopped drinking to improve my relationship and thinking." *Inner strength* is the trigger word.

- *Male Sexuality* : "I enjoy hard erection. My body performs well during sex without thinking about it. Firm erection is my natural response to sexual stimuli. During sex I maintain hard erection and delay ejaculation until I am ready. I am sexually virile and make love for long time to the full satisfaction of my partner."
- *Female Sexuality* : "My sexual desire are intense, I easily achieve an intense orgasm during sex. I enjoy sex and respond openly and joyously to my partner. My orgasm are intense and I come easily."

- *Relationship Improvement* : "My relationship with people is getting better and better. I openly communicate and share myself. I communicate directly and honestly. I accept others as they are without expectations. I experience good relationship, excitement and joy with people around me."

- *Emotional detachments* : "I mentally detach myself from negative people. I detach myself from everything that does not work for me. Negativity flows through me without affecting me.

I draw joyous new experiences in my life. I am optimistic and confident about my future." Use *detach* as trigger word.

- *Concentration* : "Total concreation is mine. I have the power and ability to focus my concentration at will. I remain alert and focussed. I easily block thoughts related to what I am working on. My goal of super concentration is easily achieved." Use *concentrate* as a trigger word.

The above affirmations are time tested and have been used successfully to solve problems and enhance performance. The success rate depends on how much one practices. One must practice daily for at least 10-15 minutes in the early morning otherwise just before going to sleep since that is the time we are cut off from the world.

The same affirmations can be used on others when you are hypnotising them by changing the 'I' to 'You'. For example, after hypnotising the person and taking him or her to at least the second stage of hypnosis, one should give the affirmations 3-5 times for it to be effective. The deeper you take a person the more effective and faster results can be obtained by positive affirmations.

For example for 'fear and worry' say, "You are a confident person and secure. You are a calm and an optimistic person. You feel powerful and in full control of yourself. You are peaceful, harmonious and balanced. Your mind is calm and thinks positive thoughts. You are in full control of your life."

Precautions and Preconditions to Hypnosis

Hypnosis is an art and an art cannot be taught but it has to be caught. All hypnotist know that hypnosis means self-hypnosis and they are only an instrument in bringing about an alpha state of mind to their subject by creating a right atmosphere and monotonous suggestions to bypass the critical factor.

Actually, we all keep hypnotising ourselves at least 15 –20 times a day when we indulge in activities like watching TV continuously. Sometimes gaping at the set with our mouth open when something interesting is being shown in rapt attention.

Any monotonous sequence of events make them boring for the brain and eventually it starts producing a hormone called serotonin which induces an alpha or drowsy state of mind. We are all living a life of a robot, a mechanical life which is very frustrating. Such frustration is an indication to 'Go forward' but where is the big question. It could be a change in our job, venturing into a new hobby or developing new skills which could be something as simple as starting to read.

The preconditions to hypnosis are:

- Congenial environment with no extreme temperature.
- Soothing background music
- Faith in the hypno-therapist
- Fixation of attention
- Progressive relaxation
- Removing all prejudices and myths about hypnosis.

A congenial environment for hypnosis is very important because all our five senses become hyperactive under hypnotic condition hence strong smells or extreme emotions should be avoided while attempting hypnosis. Room should be free from insects and dust as all of these could pose as hurdles preventing the subject from going into deep trance.

Soothing subliminal or alpha music should be used to make the subconscious mind of the subject receptive to Hypno-therapist's suggestions as these suggestions help people to go into a deeper trance.

Faith in the hypno-therapist is the prime condition. It is very important for hypnotists to form a rapport with their subject by presenting a very pleasant demeanor and displaying a genuine concern for the client's problems. Any kind of manipulation or greed alerts the auto pilot in the client's subconscious mind which says, "Don't trust this person". Clients may ask for reference from the hypnotist, if in doubt, to reconcile their faith and ensure that they are not in the hands of a quack.

Fixation of attention to backward counting or going down the staircase (described later) is the best way to bore the brain as our mind does not want to rest even for a second and is always up to tricks all the time. One can fix one's mind on breathing or an object or a moving pendulum depending on what the hypnotist prefers. It is found that the pendulum is very effective in hypnotising people for the first time.

Progressive relaxation is the key to all hypnosis. Some people may know to relax themselves if they are in the habit of practising yoga or meditations for many years. Highly stressed people have their sympathetic nervous system always on alert resulting in stress related diseases. Progressive relaxation is like "Shavasana" in yoga in which we relax each and every muscle of our body right from the feet to the tip of the head physically and mentally affirming:

"My feet are totally relaxed."

"My shin muscles are totally relaxed"

"My thighs are totally relaxed" and so on.

Any auto suggestion would result in the subconscious carrying out the orders immediately. Removing pre-conceived concepts is very important before attempting to hypnotise anyone. Often there are doubts regarding the hypnotic session as our movies have depicted how the subject literally dance to the tune of hypnotist. Thus tarnishing the image of this excellent science — hypnosis.

The technique of "Conversational Clinic" is used to understand and form a rapport with the client through the art of communication using effective persuasive words or other forms of pleasing non-verbal language. By logically removing all fears and misconceptions of hypnosis rapport can be developed with the client. The subject can be taken deeper into subconsicous level to get best results.

We have given the preconditions above, even precautions are important while using techniques of hypnosis. Hypnotist can get into serious trouble if he overlooks certain factors of the patients' health condition related to:

- Heart condition
- Hysterical behaviour
- Rape fantasy
- Neurotic behaviour
- Oversensitive subjects

It is very important to know the subject's medical background like heart condition and other psychological disorders because under hypnosis due to visualisations and affirmations it is possible that blood pressure may go up or come down drastically creating situation of instant heart attack. One should investigate thoroughly the medical history of the subject by asking a series of questions and deducing the deep inner motivating factor for hypnosis as it gives clues to the therapist. In case the client starts feeling uncomfortable or moans or displays a back and forth swing of the torso, it is a signal that he is feeling uneasy and one should bring him or her out of hypnosis immediately.

Hysterical behaviour can be treated by conversing with the subject. It is advisable to attempt hypnosis after 2-3 meetings with the patient. Extreme mood swings should be carefully observed specially during the initial meetings.

Neurotic and oversensitive people can become violent under hypnosis causing both material and physical harm to the hypnotist. This could be very embarrassing. If the client is questioned regarding the kind of medication undertaken the hypnotist would know whether the client is under treatment for neurosis It is better to avoid the hypnosis session with such subjects. Thorough knowledge of mental illnesses and their medications would be an additional asset to the hypnotists. They can also take the help of a clinical psychologist.

Some of the oversensitive humans could be great actors. They might be able to easily show extreme emotions during a simple conversation. When they are asked to recall a funny incident they may laugh abnormally or when asked to recall a sad incident they might weep uncontrollably. Hypnosis involves a lot of visualisation and constant recall of past lives and events. It might be ideal not to indulge in such cases as any attempt to either hypnotise or teach hypnosis to such folks might produce poor results.

Some of the legal requirements are that the practitioner should have at least 3-4 years of clinical experience, he or she should be a psychotherapist or should have completed a course in medical hypnosis or a course in human science. Since most clients are gullible and do not check the credentials of therapists by doing this they are inviting more harm than good for themselves. In the USA and some other countries, one has to be a registered or be a licensed practitioner failing which the compensations they are required to pay could be a very heavy sum. Best would be to ask for references about the hypnotist.

Prechecks to Hypnosis

It should be understood well that nobody can hypnotise a subject against his or her will and all hypnosis are basically "Self-hypnosis". Unless the person agrees and is ready to experience hypnotic condition it is not worthwhile attempting any hypnosis method on the subject.

It is believed that around 80–85% of people can be hypnotised and the remaining 15–20% of the population cannot be hypnotised because of various reasons like:

- Fear of hypnosis due to the myths
- Inability to relax
- No trust in the hypnotist
- Posture related problems
- Doubting attitude

All the myths and misconceptions about hypnosis should be clarified to the subjects so as to make them feel at ease about being hypnotised. Some people just cannot relax and they keep on moving their arms or legs due to anxiety or hormonal disturbance. Such people can be taught simple relaxation techniques like deep breathing, Savasana(a powerful asana in yoga), and simple meditations prior to attempting hypnosis. Self-help cassettes consisting guided progressive relaxation techniques could also be very helpful.

Faith in the hypnotist is absolutely essential because the subject will try to come out of the hypnotic trance causing hindrance to the treatment. Faith in the hypnotist could be gained by carefully observing the certificates displayed by the hypnotist at his clinic or any other testimonials of value may be made available for the information of the visitors. Hypnotist could also learn the technique of forming instant rapport with the client perhaps by mirroring the client's actions, voice tone and breathing rhythm. He should be sincere in his approach as any kind of manipulation would put the client's subconscious mind on a red alert. Rapport is the precondition to any hetero-hypnosis.

Posture related problems are when people are seated on the chair and they start to fall on their sides under hypnotic condition which will bring them out of hypnosis immediately. The best posture would be to make the subject lie down on the bed. It is difficult to hypnotise too logical and argumentative people.

3 laws or principles of hypnosis:
- Law of concentrated attention
- Law of reverse effect
- Law of repetition

We often tend to gape with our mouth open whenever we see anything interesting on the TV or cinema. This is a form of HYPNOSIS. We are not aware of anything around us. The classical dance describes this RASA as "ADHABUDHA RASA" which means wonder. Hence to bring about any hypnotic condition the subject is required to have the concentrated attention.

Law of reversed effect says that the harder we try the more difficult it becomes and this is true even when it comes to earning money. Whenever there is a conflict between imagination and will-power, the imagination wins. In hypnosis, we use this technique to give affirmation like, "Try to raise your hands, the harder you try the more difficult it will become". In our daily conversation also we should not use words like " I WILL TRY TO DO IT" as this gives a suggestion to the subconscious of a pre-failure.

Repetition is the mother of all habits as all repetitions, verbal or action and thought process are responsible for what happens on the physical plane. This phenomena is used by advertising companies very effectively by bombarding our subconscious with repeated, monotonous copies viz. "Eat Kit Kat or drink Limca" and we subconsciously tend to eat and drink those brands to which we get subconsciously conditioned.

Few tests to check the suitability or receptivity of the subject are important before deeper trance is attempted. Anyone of these tests when carried out successfully would mean that the subject is a good hypnotic subject and can be hypnotised.

• **Arm Raising and Falling Test**: Subjects are made to bring the palms of both hands parallel to the ground with the right palm facing upwards and left palm facing the floor. Ask them to close their eyes and imagine a heavy book on the right palm and a gas balloon tied to the left palm. Affirmations repeated 3-4 times would be, "Your right arm is becoming heavier and heavier and your left palm is becoming lighter and lighter. The left palm is going up and up and right palm is coming down, down, down' in a very soothing voice. The subject's imagination will run wild and their palms would be at different levels when they come out of the alpha state. The distance between the left and right palm will be considerable provided they do it gradually. A good hypnotic subject can be easily hypnotised whereas those whose imagination is poor or who are consciously keeping their arms tight would indicate a difficult hypnotic subject or may be these are the people who are just not interested.

• **Forward and Backward Falling Test**: The subject is made to stand up and the therapist stands behind the subject by resting his hands on the subject's back. The hypnotist tells the subject to close his eyes and imagine a haystack behind him. Affirmations are given, "You are absolutely comfortable and relaxed. You are now falling back on the haystack as soon as I remove my hand. Do not be afraid of falling as I am there to support you." A good subject falls immediately and care should be taken to hold quickly lost they injure themselves.

• **Glue Hand Clasp Test**: The subject is made to imagine that he or she has put a strong glue on their palms and their clasped palms are locked. Affirmations given are, "Now you are squeezing your hands tighter and tighter and as you tighten your hands the glue is becoming dry and hard. At the count of three you will try to open your hands and you will not be able to do so. The harder you try the more difficult it will become." Now unless you command that "Now you can open your palms", they will not be able to open their clasped palms. However this exercise works only for 70 – 75% of the people not everyone.

• **Eyeball Test** : The subject is made to sit down and constantly stare at the swaying pendulum or at the stationary palm of the therapist to fix his attention. Affirmations given are, "As you observe your eyelids are becoming heavier and heavier and you are getting deeply relaxed. At the count of three you will close your eyes and go into deep state of relaxation." After he closes his eyes say, " Now your eyelids are stuck and you will be unable to open them till I tell you, the harder you try the more difficult it will become." If they are unable to do so they are good subjects.

The trick in this sequence is rapport, trust, affirmations and taking the affirmations literally. Care should be taken to give affirmations such as, "Now you can open your eyelids and they are perfectly normal as before" to undo the affirmations, "you cannot open your eyelids Do not forget." Otherwise the subject continues to stay as per the instructions given during the hypnosis.

Different Methods of Hypnosis

The basic methods of hypnosis involves progressive relaxation, affirmations, are programming using different positive affirmations and creative visualisation. Once the subject is induced into hypnosis, it is very easy to take them second time provided you include trigger words like, "Every time you go into hypnosis you will go even more deeper into the deep state of relaxation and when I say sleep now you will go into deep relaxation instantly." The purpose and goal of taking the subject into hypnosis should be very clear before attempting the exercise of hypnosis.

Some of the other methods are:

• **Chevreul's Pendulum Method**: Here a pendulum made out of brass, non metal or crystal is used. The person is made to follow the sway of the pendulum keeping it about one feet away from the eyes and 6 inches above direct gaze. Suggestions like, "As you observe the pendulum swing, your eyes will become heavier and heavier and at the count of three you shall close your eyes and go into a deep state of relaxation" are given. Most probably the subjects would blink at the beginning but eventually their eyes would become tired and they would not be able to keep the eyes fixed on the swinging object. This would result in hypnosis. Even after they close their eyes it is very important to keep on saying, " With very breath you are becoming more and more relaxed and going deeper and deeper into a total state of relaxation" otherwise the subject could come out easily.

• **Gaze Fixation**: Subject can be made to fix his gaze on a shiny object held 2 feet away or at the palm of the therapist or even at the eyes of the hypnotist. Once the fixation is complete affirmations like, "As you observe the object or my eyes (whichever is applicable) you are becoming more and more relaxed, your breathing is becoming deeper. Your eyelids are becoming more and more heavier and you are going into total relaxation".

This is a powerful method and the hypnotist while asking someone to look into his eyes might sometimes get hypnotised which is exactly the reverse of what the hypnotist intended.

This ability can be strengthened by practicing Yogic technique — *Trataka* which involves observing a candle for 10-15 minutes daily without blinking the eyes or till tears roll down. This makes the person very powerful with piercing eyes and most of the people will not be able to see into your eyes. Trataka can also be practiced by constantly gazing at the moon and the early morning sun to increase psychic powers.

• **Hyperventilation Technique**: This is an old technique used by the hypnotists in the last century where the subject is made to take a deep breath and hold it for some time and then made to exhale rapidly. Due to fast exhalation carbon dioxide levels decrease leading to dizziness. The hypnotist says, "As you breathe in and out your head will become lighter and lighter". Further subsequent deepening affirmations can be given.

• **Placebo Technique**: For difficult clients this is a disguised technique where a sugar pill is given to the subject and is told, " As you take this special hypnotic pill, you will start feeling drowsy and sleepy". Say it 2-3 times in a soothing, polite demeanor since some clients do not like authoritative affirmations. After

30 minutes observe the subject and affirm" Your eyes are red and you are going into a deep state of relaxation, you are hardly able to keep your eyes open". Generally they go into a deep state of relaxation immediately.

• **Hand Levitation Method**: This can be done by instructing the subject to keep their eyes fixed on any object in front of them as described before (refer to gaze fixation) and affirm, "As you watch the object your right hand is becoming lighter and lighter. Just brush away all thoughts from your mind and shift all your focus on the object and without any effort your right palm will become lighter and lighter as if it is tied to a gas balloon and move towards your face. When it touches your cheeks it will drop down with a thud as if a wet cloth is thrown on the floor and you will close your eyes and go into deep state of relaxation". Affirmations have to be continuously said as it takes 15–20 mins to achieve this. Patience and endurance on the part of the hypnotist is the key to success of this method.

• **Three Finger Technique**: The subject is made to close his eyes and the hypnotist places his thumb on the centre of the forehead between the eyebrows (third eye) and 2 fingers on the skull. He then gives the affirmation, "As you put all your focus on your forehead your breathing is becoming deeper and deeper and you are going into a state of deep relaxation". Once the subject is under trance he can be taken deeper by further giving him suggestions to visualise a ten-flight staircase and affirming, "With every step you will go deeper and deeper into the trance. The hypnotist can even start counting backwards from 10-1 slowly and simultaneously affirming that with every count the subject will go deeper and deeper. All the muscles are getting relaxed making the subject feel heaviness in the arms, legs and other parts of the body. These suggestions would make the technique very effective.

If a blue coloured light is lit in the room where hypnosis is conducted, it helps to induce the alpha state of mind much faster and quicker.

Practical Uses of Hypnosis

"God cures and the doctor sends the bill."
-Mark Twain

The practical uses of hypnosis can be better apprehended when we understand the mind-body link. It is this link which is the basis of all psychosomatic disorders. "Psycho" means mind "Soma" means body. This makes the body and mind, part and parcel of the same system.

The figure indicates that the brain is connected to the three important systems:

Mind-body Link And The Immune System

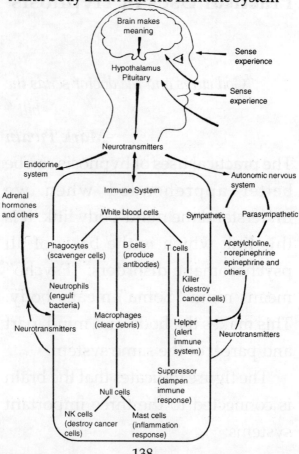

- Endocrine system — the basis of all hormones in our body
- Immune system – protects us from the attack of bacteria and virus.
- Autonomous nervous system which is sub-divided into sympathetic and parasympathetic system.

The sympathetic system puts us in a state of readiness or alertness to meet any challenges during which adrenaline, thyroxin, nurepinephrine are released resulting in increased heart beat and breathing rate, our digestion is cut off and acid secretion increases in our stomach that in turn results in anxious feelings. This is the state of stress which is good if we have to perform on stage or indulge in sport activity but remaining in stressful state always results in problems.

A parasympathetic system is just the opposite. It lowers our pulse rates and breathing resulting in comfort, relaxation and ultimately sleep. Nerve endings release endorphins and neuropeptides that makes us feel pleasant.

The endocrine system converts our thoughts into action, hence when we are in a bad mood we tend to react very fast.

When there is no ecological balance between positive and negative hormones or "Purusha" and "Prakruti" we tend to make our own lives miserable.

The autonomic nervous system, endocrine and immune system are intertwined. They exchange informations through neurotransmitters made of proteins. The immune system listens to our emotions through its own neuropeptide receptors and transmits the same to the brain via the neurotransmitters, which reacts to immune responses.

It is thus very clear that everything starts with the thought process that creates emotions, which in turn results in a motion. This is the fundamental thing to be distinctly borne in our mind. There are innumerable references in Ayurveda and ancient Chinese literature wherein mention has been made as to how pregnant women were made to listen to soothing music, smell fragrant aroma, see beautiful scenery, touch and feel pure things. In other words they were made to use all the five senses to the optimum positive level for the utmost benefit of the progeny. It was also strongly believed that the thought process even during conception of a child was important.

The immune system has two methods of defending the body, first is the cell-mediated immunity in which specialised cells recognise what is not part of the body and disposes it off directly. The second is humoral immunity where it produces antibodies to destroy specific antigens such as bacteria. The immune system is our seventh sense or the "Sense of Self". Building sense of self strengthens the immune system.

Dada Vaswani said, "Unwise people blame others, partially wise blame themselves and wise people blame no one. They take everything as it is, as an experience". You should no longer be a victim of events as you have more choice and control over your experience. Life is a balance between who we are and who we are becoming. Swamiji says, " We are running to become somebody for the fear of being nobody". Thus it is pertinent to live in the present and god is nothing but existence and presence.

How Ideas Affect Organs And Glands

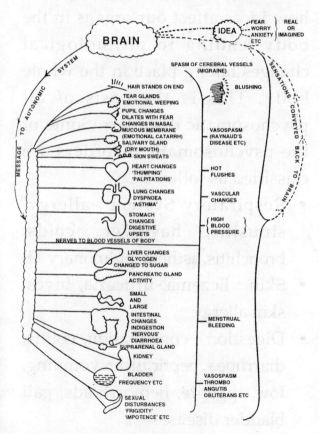

It is very clearly indicated here how ideas affect our organs in the body leading to physiological changes taking place in the whole body. This is the basis of all psychosomatic disorders. Some of the psychosomatic disorders are classified as follows:

- Respiratory System : allergy, sinusitis, hayfever, colds, bronchitis, asthma, pulmonary TB
- Skin : Eczema, urticaria, hives, skin allergy
- Digestion : constipation, colitis, diarrhoea, peptic ulcer, vomiting, low appetite, hemorrhoids, gall bladder diseases

- Vascular : high blood pressure, Reynaud's disease
- Urinary: bed wetting, nervousness urgency and incontinence.
- Nervous : alcoholism, migraine, drug addiction, diabetes mellitus, goiter, hypoglycemia, myasthenia gravis
- Genital : male – impotence, premature ejaculation, retrograde ejaculation. Female – frigidity, vaginitis, menstrual cramps and difficulties.

It is thus believed that 90% of all diseases are psychosomatic. Disease is 'disturbed ease'. When our ease either at physical, mental, emotional or spiritual level is disturbed, it results in a disease as all the disease is teaching us some lesson but our EGO (Edging God Out) does not permit us to accept the same. When we learn the lessons the disease also leaves the body; ' When the going gets tough, the tough gets going'.

Hypnosis is neither a panacea nor a be all and end all solution to all the problems nor does it replace medical help in all the above listed diseases. However, it is an additional tool in reaching normalcy. All sufferings aim to bring us back to normalcy and in harmony with GOD (Generator Operator Destroyer).

There are emotional reasons for diseases. We attract all kinds of situations in our life. If we are intrinsically good we are bound to meet only our type of people and if we are intrinsically bad or have negative thoughts hovering around us then we will attract everything negative in this world. "Like attracts like" is nothing but "Odic Force" in scientific terms.

Related Techniques and Therapies

"Certain indeed is death for the born and certain is birth for the dead, therefore over the inevitable Thou shouldst not grieve."

– *Gita 2:27*

• **Automatic Writing:** This is a very powerful method of communicating with your subconscious. Late Mrs Anita Muhl did extensive work on automatic writing. The subject is taken into a deep state of hypnosis after a series of affirmation and relaxation procedure. A pen and notepad is also given to the subject. The subject writes down the answers that he or she would ask mentally to the subconscious mind. The hands move automatically. Sometimes one would even write very legibly or in a totally different handwriting all together which does not belong to the subject at all.

One could easily practice the techniques of automatic writing. The only thumb rule to be kept in mind is that the questions should be pertaining to the present and not the future like. 'Will I become a doctor?' when the subject has no aptitude or desire to do hard work to achieve the goal he may not reap a very encouraging answer. Even insignificant questions like, 'When will I die?' will bear no fruitful answer. All questions should be about the present, 'Are my current meditations in tune with my spiritual growth? How can I become more useful to this world? 'What are the hobbies and interest I should pursue?', etc.

• **Pendulum:** Pendulum could be made of acrylic, brass or crystal It is a useful tool to communicate with our subconscious mind. The pendulum could be stringed at one end and programmed as under :

The pendulum should be kept in hand and swung vertically and one should mentally repeat 'yes', 'yes', 'yes'... 10 times. The resource for the pendulum is your subconscious mind and hence what is in the subconscious only will answer correctly otherwise it will give wrong readings.

Pendulums can be used for:

- Selecting medicines good for you and others. A very useful tool for homeopaths as it helps them to select best out of many logical choices.
- Knowing the condition of the patient.

- Finding directions like east, west, north, south.
- Finding energies in different places of the house. Useful tool for Vastu/Feng Shui and for people who use it for correcting energies in different corners and locations.
- Selecting the right life partner or business associate.

It is important to note that answers given by pendulum are only indicative and all logical procedure need to be followed for taking the final decision.

• **Past Life Regression:** The very thought of regressing into the past may seem scary to many.

Subconscious mind has a permanent memory of events that have occurred either in this life or in the previous lives. The conscious mind rejects most of the happenstance save those that are major or traumatic, that leave more or less a permanent scar on the subconscious. You may have noticed that there are some people whom you meet for the first time and you abhor them for no known reason. Here the subconscious mind remember some incident relating to that person and triggers the signal of non-acceptance or dislike. Even the reverse happens that is some people whom you meet might instantly become your friends. They might have been your friends from the past lives and the subconscious has been able recognise to them. Past life regression is a journey back in time in the present life or past life using the power of your subconscious to basically change our perception of life. This is an enlightenment process to understand who we are and the deeper meaning in being incarnated being in this body. It is an audio-visual experience in which we see a set of scenes and sounds or even feel certain feelings related to the past of this life or past lives. This becomes possible due to the superior intelligence of the subconscious and also its willingness to view these incidences.

Generally, past life regression is used for traumatic and unusual experiences that have no logic or medical experiences.

A word of caution here is that the subject is bound to view these events as real experience at the physical level. It will certainly help the subject if the Hypnotherapist says that the event is being viewed by the subject as a witness and not as a victim.

Regression therapy is a specialised job and unless the hypnotist is experienced he should not even try it.

Similar to the past life regression it is also possible to go into future life regression. Some people argue that it could basically be our imagination but the fact remains that our mind cannot even imagine what is not possible. Had it not been for the imagination of the Wright brothers there would have been no airplanes today. As per Albert Einstein, 'There is no past, no future; everything is happening simultaneously but in a different dimension.

- **Neuro Linguistic Programming (NLP):** NLP is a relatively new science which studies our structure of subjective experiences and creates an unique internal world to experience the external world. This is a powerful science invented by Dr Richard Brandler and John Grinder in the 70's.

Neuro refers to the Neurology and shows how body and mind are linked through the nervous system. Linguistic is the language aspect; both verbal and non-verbal (body language and eye cues).

Programming is the repeated sequences of thoughts and behaviour how we act to gain our goals and the consequence of our own action. NLP is a body of ideas and our way of thinking and is about enriching our own model of anything be it health, communication skills, selling, etc. This in turn helps you to look for answers within.

NLP has many techniques to change our perception about health, goals, beliefs and values system, fears and phobias, allergies, modern medicine even involving mild hypnosis and visualisation techniques.

Some cases treated by using Hypnosis.

• **Low Self Esteem**: Miss Dechemma, a 23 year old girl, came to us for treatment. She was suffering from poor self-image and constant depression although she had no real cause of worry in her life. She had a mild traumatic experience when she was about 10 years as her peers in school used to make fun of her. This had got embedded deep in her subconscious and she believed herself to be the biggest fool on earth.

After counseling we informed her that it was her perception of things around her which was not true at all. She was taught self-hypnosis and techniques of complete mental reprogramming by simple affirmations alongwith subliminal music which made her 60% better. However, the memory of her experience was still there. A past life regression was done and the whole incident of the past was erased which made her stand on her own legs and have definite goals in life. She was also taught Reiki to keep her energies high and overcome stress levels.

- **Alcohol Addictions**: Another patient was addicted to alcohol for over 15 years and he wanted to leave it but did not know how to do it. During the normal healing he was taken into hypnosis and a set of affirmations for alcohol and depressions were given which helped him to come out of the constant urge for alcohol. He was taught visualisation techniques for a daily practice.

- **Impotence**: Mr R a businessman, never enjoyed marital bliss due to his bad experiences encountered with hired sex partners. Energy healing with affirmations suggested under hypnotic state brought about improved relationship with his spouse. The holistic treatment given to him included nutritious diet, yogic breathing exercises, aerobic exercises viz. walking, counseling, and spiritual healing.

• **Hole in the Heart:** Miss Vijay Lakshmi had a congenital hole in the heart which impaired her routine activities and lead to difficulty in leading a normal life. She often suffered tiredness and breathlessness, cough and cold. Energy healing and creative visualisation techniques helped her to attain a better quality life. She is on a better road to recovery and has more or less forgotten all about her ailment.

• **Cancer patient:** A patient, carrying the lymph gland (Non-Hodgkin) cancer, had to go through chemotherapy, radiography and other treatments repeatedly. Finally due to lack of adequate platelet count in his bone marrow he was unable to continue further treatment. Physically and mentally drained of all energy he resigned himself to wait for his end. He had lost all interest in eating, communicating with his family and friends. On undergoing energy healing and creative visualisation techniques, he became more positive about getting better and better. Three months later he even started driving around, going for shopping and eating better food. In other words it was like a rebirth.

• **Partial Paralysis:** Mrs ABC was becoming partially paralysed due to poor nervous co-ordination and nerve weakness due to unexplained reasons. She was repeatedly told to visualise how she was before suffering from this illness i.e. before she got the stroke. These affirmations coupled with the energy healing gave tremendous improvement to her physical condition as she.

- **Stress Problem:** Several patients have also been treated for stress problem resulting in depression and further culminating into nicotine or alcohol dependence that leads to further problems. Apart from healing they were taught autohypnosis and affirmations, which gave them total independence, and which put them in control of the situation instead of the situation being in control of them.
- **Allergic Reactions:** Allergies like asthma, food allergy, skin dermatitis are very tricky and modern medicine is offering very little to solve these oilments. Energy healing with NLP, mild hypnosis and visualisation with

affirmations can help the patient to boost his immune system.

All the patients continued their allopathic treatment as well although some brought down the intake of medicines visits to the doctor and subsequent because they all experienced a sense of well being and good health. Holistic approach of combining mind power through hypnosis and the universal energy through various energy(spiritual) healing methods have been giving very valuable results in bringing about a permanent relief from most all the ailments.